Dear Children

The Heaven's Flowers To Make The Paradise

S Afrose

Ukiyoto Publishing

All global publishing rights are held by

Ukiyoto Publishing

Published in 2023

Content Copyright © S Afrose

ISBN 9789359202150

*All rights reserved.
No part of this publication may be reproduced,
transmitted, or stored in a retrieval system, in any form
by any means, electronic, mechanical, photocopying,
recording or otherwise, without the prior permission of
the publisher.*

The moral rights of the authors have been asserted.

*This is a work of fiction. Names, characters, businesses,
places, events, locales, and incidents are either the
products of the author's imagination or used in a fictitious
manner. Any resemblance to actual persons, living or
dead, or actual events is purely coincidental.*

*This book is sold subject to the condition that it shall not by
way of trade or otherwise, be lent, resold, hired out or
otherwise circulated, without the publisher's prior
consent, in any form of binding or cover other than that in
which it is published.*

www.ukiyoto.com

To the dearest, most favourite, Little one-"ADYAN"
May Almighty bless you always, dear.
May Almighty bless you always with sound health, for the beautiful life.

Acknowledgement

I am so much grateful…To Dear Almighty! "You always help me"

Thanks!
Dear parents!
"Without their supports, I can't move on or stand up smoothly"

Thanks!
Dear friends!
"Without their love towards my writes, I am bound to lose myself"

Thanks!
Dear readers!
"They love my words. And I am so much grateful for this love"

From Author Desk
S Afrose
Dhaka, Bangladesh, 2nd Sep-23.

Essence Of The Poetry Garden

Children are angels. They are heaven's flowers. We love them. When a child comes into a home, that's turned into the paradise, instantly.

Parents feel it. A special fragrance of life starts. So beautiful. Nothing can beat this part. Parents love children always. They try the best, for their happiness. They can do anything for the wellness of the children.

This book contains so many writes, containing the emotions of parents and children. As for example- Happy, Birthday, Little fairy, Baby, Dear Child, Share and Care, A to B etc.

Each one reflects a core message. Some come from the child, some come from the parents. Over all, the emotion flows to show the world- dear children, make the paradise; when they came into a tiny hut.

But, they need to realize the fact,

Parents are the best friends. They must obey their words. They must love them, unconditionally.

Hold this book and spend some nice moments. I think so. For any kind of unexpected word, just forgive.

Thanks!
From Author desk.
S Afrose
Bangladesh
2nd Sep-23

"Let's make the ride
of the beautiful realm
of words"

Contents

Happy	1
Birthday	2
The Party	3
The Beautiful Dress	4
Little Fairy	5
Baby	6
Something Else	7
I Dare To Say	8
I Will Love You Dear	9
Flowers On Earth	10
You Are Not Alone	11
Brother-Sister	12
See And Then Say	13
Be	14
A Mug Of Milk	15
Your Favourite One	16
Dear Child	17
Dear Child 2	19

On This Day	20
Why Do You Cry?	21
Wash	23
Breakfast	24
Play On The Play time	25
Listen Your Teachers	26
Listen Your Parents	27
A Gift	28
Share Your Tiffin	29
Share And Care	30
The Favourite Show	31
A to B	32
C to D	33
E to F	34
G to H	35
The Reading Table	36
Little Children	37
Children And Parents	38
Angels	41
See My Art	42

The Sweet Hub	43
Your Smile	44
I to J	45
K to L	46
M to N	47
My Books	48
Cupboard	49
You Are A Super Hero	50
O to P	51
Q to R	52
S to T	53
U to V	54
W to X	55
Y to Z	56
Morning Calling	57
Time For The School	58
Good Evening	59
Good Night	60
About the Author	62

Happy

Happy!
So happy!
The sun, the moon,
And the galaxy.

Happy!
So happy!
Waiting,
Till the end of lane.

Happy! We are so happy!
As this is the blessing boon for us.
You came on this day my dear.
Happy birthday!

(30th Aug-23)

Dear Children

Birthday

It's the most beautiful day.
I can see so many colours,

I get so many gifts.
There's a lot of fun.

So many friends!
So many guests!

A beautiful and delicious cake!
I love and enjoy this day.

(30th Aug-23)

The Party

It's your day
What do you want?
Give a cute smile.
A party?

With your friends,
And your parents,
And your relatives.
The gorgeous party!

Oh Dad!
I love you,
I love you Mom.
I love the party.

(30th Aug-23)

The Beautiful Dress

Wear this part,
Your beautiful art,
The beautiful dress!

The red or white,
Blue or green
The beautiful dress!

My beautiful dress,
I love this,
Love you dear Parents.

(30th Aug-23)

Little Fairy

Little fairy smiles.
Dancing butterfly!

Little angel comes.
Smile and smell of love.

Wait for the night,
Will get the sight.

Little fairy comes
In this sweet paradise.

(30th Aug-23)

Baby

Baby O' Baby!
I love you!

Baby O' Baby!
You're my apples of eyes.

Baby O' Baby!
A little flower!

Baby O' Baby!
Heaven's shower!

(30th Aug-23)

Something Else

Nothing can change this part,
Except the most important art.

Something else.
You better chase.

How can make the race?
The holy motion is stucked.

Need the caption of love,
Something else... the lovely shower.

(30th Aug-23)

I Dare To Say

I dare to say,
This is not my beloved day.

I lost my happiness.
My mother, on this day.

How can I be happy?
As I can't stop falling tears.

My mother is not here.
Happy birthday!Damn care!

(30th Aug-23)

I Will Love You Dear

I will love you dear,
My little Princess!

I will love you dear,
My little Prince!

I will love you dear,
You must believe this.

You are my Paradise!
I will love you always.

(30th Aug-23)

Flowers On Earth

When a baby comes

Into a hut,

It turns, to the paradise.

Flowers on earth!

When a baby comes

Into the lap of parents,

That turns to the most beautiful art, instant.

Flowers on earth

For all the parts,

Of the dearest hut.

(1st Sep-23)

You Are Not Alone

Baby I am here,
Always;
You don't need to scare.
I am here,
Your dearest parents,
Mother and Father.
You are not alone dear.

Baby I am here,
You can express
Why do you cry?
We will care,
You are not alone, dear!

(1st Sep-23)

Brother-Sister

Love yourself.
Love your parents.
Love your family.
Live with love.
Love, Brother-Sister.

It brings for you
Happiness.
You will get,
The precious stage.
Don't forget that,
Love yourself.

(1st Sep-23)

See And Then Say

See it

And then say.

What will you want?

What can you see?

Make it

And then show

The world,

You can make, your own paradise.

(1st Sep-23)

Be

Be with your love,
Be with your hut,
Be with your art.

You see,
You know,
You love.

Be happy.
Be the smiley sun.
Be the adorable one.

(1st Sep-23)

A Mug Of Milk

Drink the milk,
A favourite and delicious dish,
For your health.

A mug of milk.
You will love this,
You will get the sweet taste.

Don't deny
Having the milk,
Dear child.

(1st Sep-23)

Your Favourite One

Dear child,
Which book
Is your favourite one?

Dear child,
You can share
With me.

Dear child,
Which book helps you
To smile?

I love the story book, Mom.
The fairy tales.
Just wow!

(1st Sep-23)

Dear Child

Dear child,
Which deed you love
To do?

You can say it,
I will not take in mind,
Just express.

Oh Mom!
I love to draw the world,
The nature, the bosom of earth.

That's great.
You will be a good painter.
I think so.

Love your work.

Dear Children

I will help you,
At each time.

(1st Sep-23)

Dear Child 2

Dear child!
Remember,
You have to give thanks,
To dear Almighty.

Prayer!
The best way,
To be calm
To touch the serene verse.

Surrender to dear Almighty!
Be patience,
Be quiet.
You will be a great person.

(1st Sep-23)

On This Day

On this day of earth,

You came

Into this little life.

You made

This one,

The legend of life.

On this day,

I can feel,

I can understand;

How beautiful this life!

Yes,

My dear child!

(1st Sep-23)

Why Do You Cry?

Oh!

My dear child!

Why do you cry?

What's happened?

Tell Mom.

I will try

To help you,

To heal your pain.

Oh dear Mom!

Someone hits me.

I don't know, why?

I am in the deepest ocean of pain.

Silly child!

It's fine.

He or she may be your friend.
You better make your mind.
You will be my good and smiley child.

(1st Sep-23)

Wash

Wash,

When you will come

From the outside of the home.

It will help

To be healthy,

To make you, the cheerful one.

(1st Sep-23)

Breakfast

Eat it,

Finish it,

Your favourite breakfast.

Never make

that mistake,

I don't want to eat this meal, Mom.

It's good for your health.

Mom knows,

What will be the best for your health?

(1st Sep-23)

Play On The Play time

Yes

Dear child,

Play on the playtime.

Yes

My dear child,

Play with your friends.

Yes

My dear child,

It will cheer up your mind.

(1st Sep-23)

Listen Your Teachers

Dear child
In the school,
Listen your teachers.

Dear child
Don't make a noise,
On the class time.

Dear child
Make yourself obedient,
On the road of study.

(1st Sep-23)

Listen Your Parents

Yes,

You can do that;

Just listen your parents.

Yes,

You will do that;

Just listen your parents.

Your parents,

Are your

Best friends.

(1st Sep-23)

A Gift

What do you like

To take,

From your Mom,

As a gift?

Mom!

Live with me,

Love me always.

That's the best gift for me

(1st Sep-23)

Share Your Tiffin

Share your tiffin
With your friends.
This will make
A strong connection.

Share your thoughts
With your friends,
As a knot of trust and love.

(1st Sep-23)

Share And Care

Share and care
When you will scare,
Without any tear.

Five or six,
A little tricky step.
Just love it.

Play and care,
Your dear friends.
Love it.

(1st Sep-23)

The Favourite Show

This is your favourite show,
>The Alphabet zone.

A to Z
>Give your state.

Love and respect.

This is your favourite guitar
>The Alphabet song.

You will sing
A to Z, as your sense.

(1st Sep-23)

A to B

A to B!
Apple and Bee.
Beautiful set,
I love it.

I eat apple.
I see the bee.
There's the honey bee,
I love it.

(1st Sep-23)

C to D

C to D
Cat and Doggy

I have a pet cat
Its name is Mini.

I love my doggy.
I enjoy my time with it.

I play with them
They are my friends.

(1st Sep-23)

E to F

E to F
Elephant to Fairyland.

I love to make the ride
On the Elephant.

I love to hear
All fairy tales.

(1st Sep-23)

G to H

G to H
Goat to Horse.

I have a kid of goat,
I play with it.

I have a horse.
He is my favourite Toy.

(1st Sep-23)

The Reading Table

The reading table!
Care, each of your part;
Love and love.
You are the good student,
My sweetheart!

I know you are.
You live as your own way,
Love your Mother.
Love your parents.

The reading table is here
To be with your dear,
You can't hide from its heart.

(1st Sep-23)

Little Children

Dear Little Children
You all are same,
Apples of my eyes.

Mom loves you all.
A knot of happiness,
Around us.

A pond is here.
So many flowers,
All are heaven's arts.

Little Children
Angels,
For the parents.

(2nd Sep-23)

Children And Parents

Daddy is here.
What's happened my dear?
Share and release your fear.

Daddy!
I don't know.
I need Jack's toy

I will give you
On the birthday.
Pls don't cry.

This is the chord of love,
Daddy with his child.
You can't imagine dear.

Mommy!

Where are you?
I am hungry.

Mommy is sick,
Still comes and says,
Dear sweetheart!

Just few moments more,
I will prepare your favourite dish.
You will enjoy.

O' Mommy!
You are the best.
I love you so much.

Children and Parents,
The song is heard all the time,
The most beautiful art.

Dear Children

(2nd Sep-23)

Angels

Children
Angels.

Children
Crescent lane.

Children
A beautiful garden.

Children
Heaven's essence.

(2nd Sep-23)

See My Art

My sweet Mommy,
See this art.
I have sketched,
Your portrait.

My sweet Dad,
See my write.
I have written,
A letter of love.

I love you,
Mom and Dad!
Both of you are my precious gems,
Love me always.

(2nd Sep-23)

The Sweet Hub

In this part
Only one art,
Your beautiful eyes,
The little child.

The sweet hub!
The eternal mart!

Children!
O'dear Children!
Love you all,
As our angels.

(2nd Sep-23)

Your Smile

Only your smile
Can break,
A border line
Of our happiness .

Yes dear child!
You have created,
This part
Of our lives.

Without you
We are meaningless.
You are,
The apple of our eyes.

(2nd Sep-23)

I to J

Ice-cream & Jam.

I love Ice-cream,
I love Jam.

But dear hold your motion.

Too much Ice-cream
Is not good for your health.

Jam will take
Over the slice of bread,
On the time of breakfast or snacks time.

(2nd Sep-23)

K to L

King and Lie

You are the king
Of your life.

You have to realize this fact.

Don't tell a lie.

Always
Be honest,
To you and your Almighty.

(2nd Sep-23)

M to N

Moon and New friend

I love the moon.
It smiles
At night time.

I love making new friends.

Each friend is my favourite one,
Like the Moon,
Someone is very special.

Mom- you're my best friend.

(2nd Sep-23)

My Books

I love my books.

They help me
To know so many things.

I am a little one.

I love
Learning, so many things.

I love my books
They are my favourite ones.

(2nd Sep-23)

Cupboard

It's your cupboard.

You have to decorate it,
With your goods.

Dresses or toys,
Books or gifts etc.

Whatever, you want?
Keep it nicely.

(2nd Sep-23)

You Are A Super Hero

Yes dear child,
You are a super hero.
Our sunshine!

Yes dear child,
Your each word,
Touching our minds.

We are your parents.
You are our super hero.

We love you.
We live for your happiness.

(2nd Sep-23)

O to P

Open the heart and Pigeon's love

I love
My family,
Always.

I love the pigeons.

They are very cute.
Icon of calmness shower,
Like the dreamy world.

(2nd Sep-23)

Q to R

Queen and Rainbow!

Mommy!
You are the queen.
I love you so much.

Look at the rainbow!

So many colours.
Red-Blue-Yellow,
Violet-Indigo-Green-Orange.

Each colour has its own meaning.

(2nd Sep-23)

S to T

Sun and Tree

I love the sun.
It smiles
At day time.

I love the tree.

Its green leaves
Spread fragrance
Of pure life.

(2nd Sep-23)

U to V

Up lifting mind and Violin

It's your mind.

Helps

To smile.

The violin!

Making the friendship

With it,

To restore the rhythms of life.

(2nd Sep-23)

W to X

War and X-ray!

Say this word
No war.

X-ray your thoughts.

Before saying anything
Before doing any deed.

(2nd Sep-23)

Y to Z

Youthful state and Zigzag arts!

Love and live
Within the youthful state.

Zigzag arts, everywhere.

Be careful
For making any step onward.

(2nd Sep-23)

Morning Calling

Dear child!
It's time, just wake up;
As Morning calling,
All of us.

Get up
And take the shower,
Praying for the beautiful day,
To dear Almighty, sweetheart.

(2nd Sep-23)

Time For The School

Don't make any call.
That will tell,
You are a devastated fallen ball.

It's time
For the school.
So get ready.

School is a good place.
You will meet with many friends,
Your teachers.

You will enjoy the time,
Don't forget.
So be ready, quickly.

(2nd Sep-23)

Good Evening

The sunset arrives.
You have to know,
It's the time
To be inside the home.

Outside so dark,
Will be very soon.
You're very young,
You can't be there, alone.

(2nd Sep-23)

Good Night

Good night dear.
It's time
To take the nap.
Just take it.

I will say you,
Good night!
Have a sweet dream.

Papa is also here
To say,
Good night!
Have a sweet dream.

(2nd Sep-23)

"THANK YOU SO MUCH
FOR YOUR LOVE,
TOWARDS MY TINY POETRY WORLD,
THE PARADISE OF WORDS."
© S AFROSE
BANGLADESH

About the Author

S Afrose

Author S Afrose (Sabiha Afrose, from Bangladesh) has made her writing realm since August-2020. She enjoys each of the part of this writing ward. She tries to express the hidden word or emotion, by her words; with the glamour of poetry. Poetry is her best friend. Her writes have been published on magazines and anthologies. In this writing realm, she has achieved many recognitions & awards (beyond her expectations).

Published author of poetry books- Thanks Dear God, Poetic Essence, Reflection of Mind, Glittering Hopes,

Angels Smile, Tiny Garden of Words, Dancing Alphabet, Artistic Muse, Essence of love, The Magical Quill.

All are available worldwide (on Amazon.com & from publication hub). Apart these, there are some Bengali and English poetry books (available on rokomari.com in Bangladesh).

Her mother is Selina Begum and father is Manirul Islam.

Educational achievements- B Pharm, M Pharm from Jahangirnagar University, Bangladesh..

Contact- afrosewritings@outlook.com,

sabiha_pharma@yahoo.com

You Tube: S Afrose *Muse of

Writes*(@safrose_poetic_arts)

Facebook page: Muse of words by S Afrose

Twitter:@afrose2020

Inst. @safrosepoetryworld

www.ingramcontent.com/pod-product-compliance
Lightning Source LLC
LaVergne TN
LVHW041545070526
838199LV00046B/1829